MASTER THEORY

Intermediate Harmony & Arranging Workbook

by Charles S. Peters and Paul Yoder

The Fifth Workbook in the MASTER THEORY SERIES

Contents

ISBN 0-8497-0158-9

CHORD POSITION

The TONIC (I), SUBDOMINANT (IV) and DOMINANT (V) TRIADS are known as the PRINCIPAL CHORDS in any key. (Review Lessons 1, 9 and 23 in Book 4, Master Theory "Elementary Harmony")

When the notes of a chord are written as close together as possible, the chord is said to be in CLOSE POSITION.

(A) Principal Chords in the Key of C Major, in Close Position

When the notes of a chord are spread beyond the closest possible intervals, the chord is said to be in OPEN POSITION.

(B) Principal Chords in the Key of C Major, in Open Position

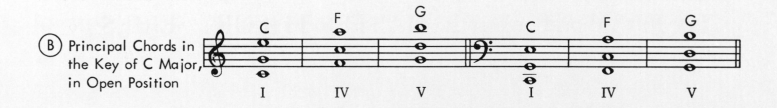

In major keys the Principal Chords are all MAJOR TRIADS. In minor keys the Tonic (I) and Subdominant (IV) are MINOR TRIADS, while the Dominant (V) is a MAJOR TRIAD.

(C) Principal Chords in the Key of c minor, in Close Position

Minor chords are marked with small letters (c). Major chords are marked with capital letters (C).

(D) Principal Chords in the Key of c minor, in Open Position

REMEMBER:- A major triad consists of a root, major third and perfect fifth. (see MASTER THEORY Book 4, "Elementary Harmony", Lesson 1.) A minor triad consists of a root, minor third and perfect fifth. (see MASTER THEORY Book 4, Lesson 23.)

STUDENT ASSIGNMENT

In Ex. 1 write the PRINCIPAL CHORDS in CLOSE POSITION in the indicated major keys. Watch the clef signs. Write the letter name above each chord.

In Ex. 2 write the PRINCIPAL CHORDS in CLOSE POSITION in the indicated relative minor keys. Remember the major 3rd in V. Write the letter name above each chord. Major and minor keys which have the same key signature (E♭ – c) are called RELATED KEYS.

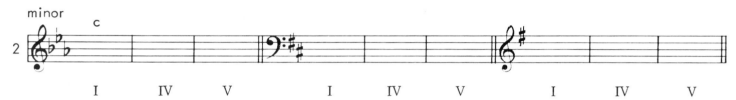

In Ex. 3 and 4 write the chords from Ex. 1 and 2 in OPEN POSITION. Write the letter name above each chord.

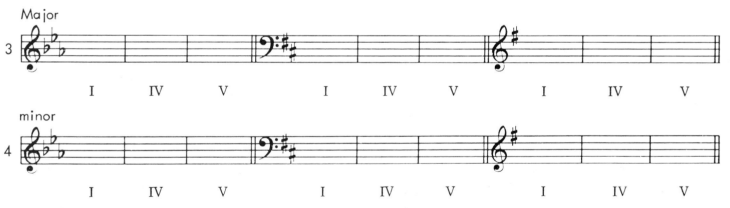

Fill in the missing note or notes in the following chords in CLOSE POSITION, with the root as the lowest note. Write the letter name above each chord. Notice the key signatures. These are not related keys as they are above.

Fill in the missing note or notes in the following chords in OPEN POSITION with the root as the lowest note. Write the letter name above each chord.

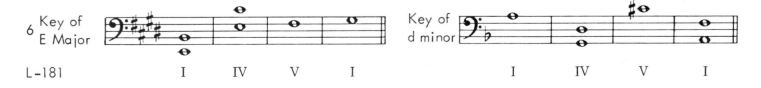

L-181

INVERSIONS

Up to this point all chords have been written in ROOT POSITION (with the root as the lowest note). When any note other than the root appears as the lowest note of the chord, it is known as an INVERSION. Numbers are placed beside the chord symbol (Roman numeral) to indicate the different inversions.

FIRST INVERSION

(A) When the third (3rd) appears as the lowest note, the chord is in the FIRST INVERSION.

The numbers $\frac{6}{3}$ spell out the intervals of the chord from the lowest note.

(B) In Ex. (A) the G is a 3rd above E. 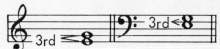 The C is a 6th above E.

(C) In common practice, the FIRST INVERSION is simply marked I₆

(D) These chords may also be written in OPEN POSITION.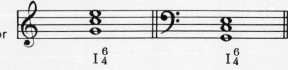

SECOND INVERSION

(E) When the fifth (5th) appears as the lowest note, the chord is in the SECOND INVERSION.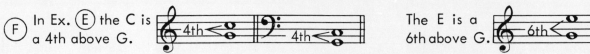

The numbers $\frac{6}{4}$ spell out the intervals of the chord from the lowest note.

(F) In Ex. (E) the C is a 4th above G.  The E is a 6th above G.

(G) SECOND INVERSION of Principal Chords in the Key of C Major.

STUDENT ASSIGNMENT

Date _____

Grade _____

Ex.1 shows the ROOT POSITION, FIRST INVERSION and SECOND INVERSION of the Principal Chords in the Key of C Major. In Ex.2, write the proper chord symbols under each, including any inversions.

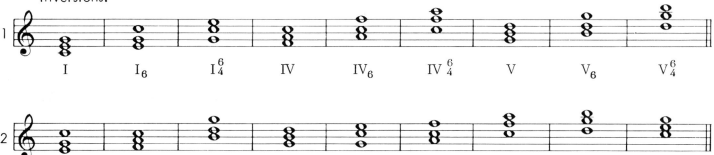

1

I I_6 I_4^6 IV IV_6 IV_4^6 V V_6 V_4^6

2

In Ex.3 and 4 write the chords in the proper inversions as indicated. Remember when there are no small numbers, the chord is in Root Position (the root is the lowest note).

Key of C Major

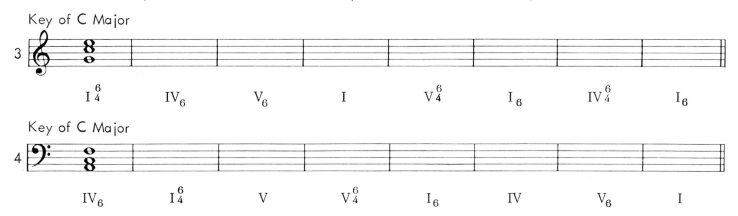

3

I_4^6 IV_6 V_6 I V_4^6 I_6 IV_4^6 I_6

Key of C Major

4

IV_6 I_4^6 V V_4^6 I_6 IV V_6 I

In Ex.5 write the chords from Ex.2 in OPEN POSITION. Write the chord symbols, including the proper inversions.

5

I_6

In Ex.6 and 7 write the chords from Ex.3 and 4 in OPEN POSITION. Write the chord symbols, including the proper inversions.

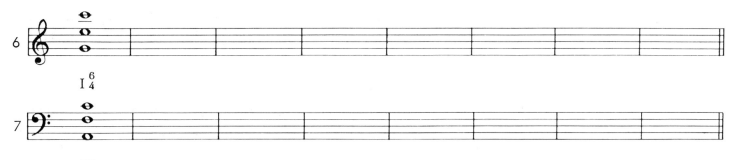

6

I_4^6

7

IV_6

HYMN TUNES

The most familiar form of four part writing is the HYMN TUNE. In most Hymns, the four voice parts – Soprano, Alto, Tenor and Bass – carry the same rhythmic values, based on the text. For this reason, it is quite easy to analyze the harmonic structure. Hymns are usually written on two staves with the Soprano and Alto parts in the Treble Clef and the Tenor and Bass parts in the Bass Clef.

Here is the harmonic analysis of the first four measures of:-

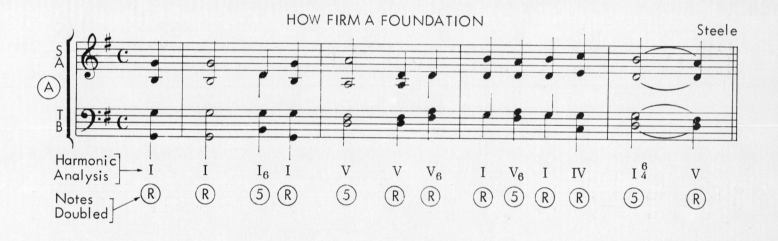

The ⓡ and ⑤ are not part of the harmonic analysis but simply show which note of the triad has been doubled to make a four part chord. ⓡ = Root doubled. ⑤ = 5th doubled.

The Third is not doubled as often as the Root or Fifth. However, the following example shows two chords with a doubled third.

STUDENT ASSIGNMENT

Date _____

Grade _____

In Ex.1 analyze the chords and write the CHORD SYMBOLS (Roman numerals) and INVERSIONS (small numbers) below the lower staff.

SOLDIERS OF THE CROSS

Webb

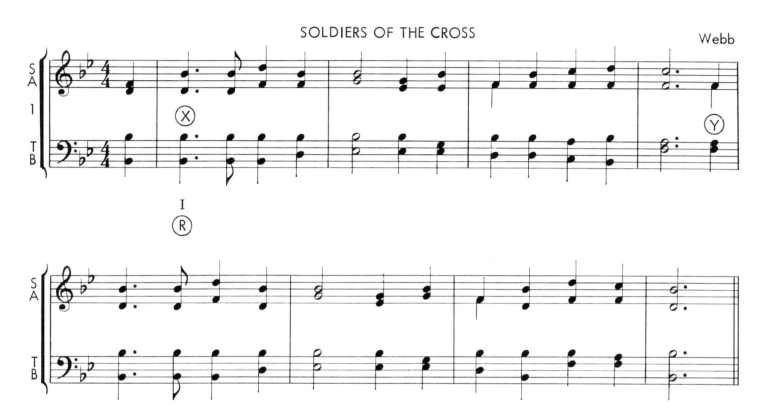

Now mark the notes which are doubled below the chord symbols. At (X) and (Y) the Root appears in three voices for smoother voice leading.

Name the interval of the chord omitted at (X) _____ (Y) _____ .

In Ex.2 fill in the Bass part (stems down) as indicated by the chord symbols. The Inversions tell you which note, other than the Root, should appear in the Bass part.

LEAD ON, O KING ETERNAL

Smart

L-181   I   I   I   IV$_4^6$ IV$_4^6$ I   I   I$_4^6$ IV$_6$ IV$_6$ I$_4^6$ IV   V

INVERSIONS OF THE DOMINANT SEVENTH CHORD (V⁷)

A DOMINANT SEVENTH CHORD consists of a Root, Major 3rd, Perfect 5th and minor 7th. In Root Position it is marked V^7 (review Lesson 11 in Book 4 Master Theory, "Elementary Harmony").

THE V^7 IN CLOSE POSITION

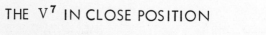

The ROOT of the V^7 chord is the 5th degree of the scale.

THE V^7 IN OPEN POSITION

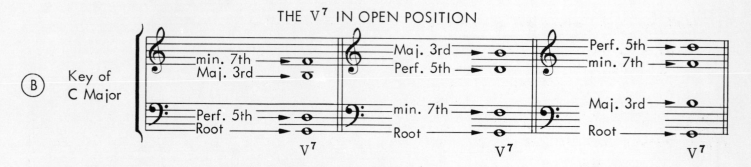

The V^7 chord may appear in Root Position as in (A) and (B) above or in any one of the three Inversions in (C). The small numbers spell out the intervals of the chord from the lowest note.

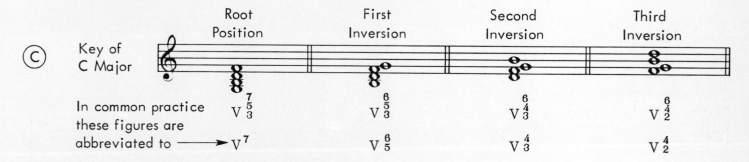

Here is a Hymn Tune containing some V^7 chords. Notice that they appear in Open Position.

ANGELS FROM THE REALMS OF GLORY

＊ 5th omitted, Root doubled.

STUDENT ASSIGNMENT

Date _____

Grade _____

In Ex. 1 write the Dominant Seventh Chords (V⁷) in CLOSE POSITION in the keys indicated. The note given in each case is the ROOT.

1

In Ex. 2 write the V⁷ Chords and the Inversions indicated, in CLOSE POSITION.

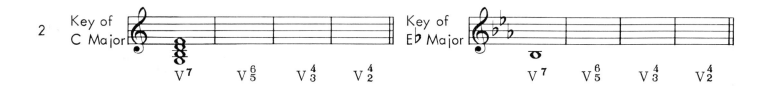

2

In Ex. 3 write the same chords in OPEN POSITION. Try to spread the intervals evenly with not more than an octave between any two voices.

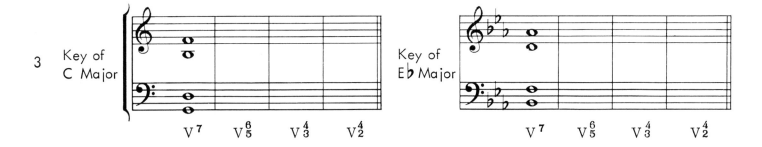

3

Analyze the harmony in the following Hymn and write in the proper chord symbols. Notice that both the V and V⁷ Chords are used. Since the V⁷ Chord contains four notes, it is not necessary to double any of the intervals.

FOR THE BEAUTY OF THE EARTH

Shaw

4

L-181   I   V⁴₃ I   V₆ I

INVERSIONS IN MINOR

(Review Lesson 23 in Book 4 Master Theory "Elementary Harmony")

If we build Triads on every degree of the Harmonic Minor Scale, we will find that the TONIC (I) and the SUBDOMINANT (IV) are MINOR CHORDS while the DOMINANT (V) is a MAJOR CHORD.

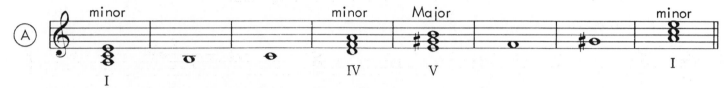

These chords may also appear in various INVERSIONS in either close or open position.

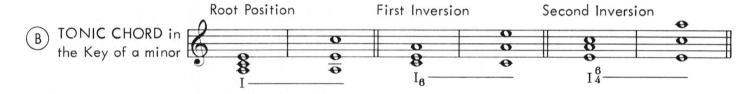

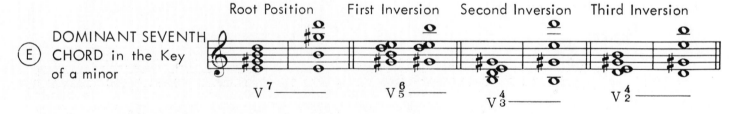

Here is an example of a Chorale for four voices in the Key of a minor. Notice the Inversions.

REMEMBER:- The triads found in this lesson are built on the harmonic minor scale. (see MASTER THEORY Book 3, Lesson 67.) The harmonic minor scale is the same both ascending and descending. Thus the raised 7th degree of this scale becomes the major third of the Dominant triad (V).

STUDENT ASSIGNMENT

Date _____

Grade _____

In Ex.1 write the proper chord symbols below, including any inversions.

In Ex. 2 and 3 write the inversions of the chords as indicated by the chord symbols. Write all chords in close position. Note the clef signs.

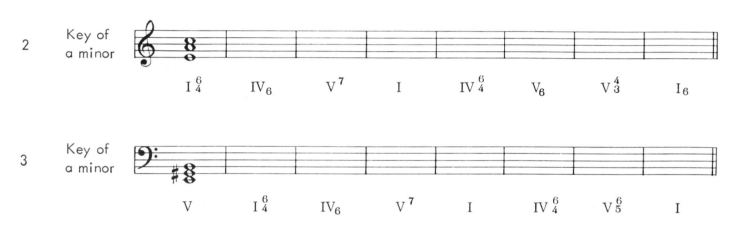

Write these chords in open position.

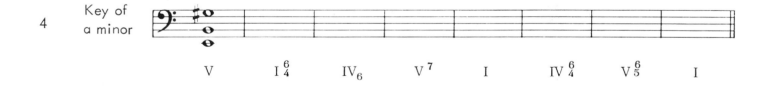

Analyze the harmony in the following Chorale and write the chord symbols below.

PART WRITING

The scale contains certain active tones which tend to move in a particular direction. The most important of these are the 4th and 7th degrees of the scale.

The 4th degree of the scale has a natural tendency to DESCEND.

The 7th degree of the scale has a natural tendency to ASCEND.

Note the movement of the 4th and 7th scale degrees in Ex. (A) .

MY FAITH LOOKS UP TO THEE

Mason

I   V₆   V⁶₅ I   V   V⁷   V⁶₅   I   V

Ex. (A) also illustrates the various types of MOTION between the parts.

 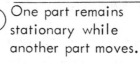
(B) **OBLIQUE MOTION** One part remains stationary while another part moves.

measure 1

(C) **CONTRARY MOTION** Parts move in opposite directions.

measure 2

(D) **PARALLEL MOTION** Parts move in same direction with the same interval.

measure 3

(E) **SIMILAR MOTION** Parts move in same direction with different intervals.

measure 4

(F) It is considered best to avoid Parallel Fifths and Parallel Octaves for the time being because these progressions tend to overemphasize the two voices involved.

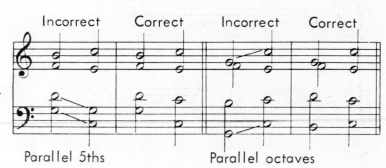
Incorrect   Correct   Incorrect   Correct

Parallel 5ths   Parallel octaves

STUDENT ASSIGNMENT

Date _____

Grade _____

In Ex. 1 write the word above each example that describes the type of MOTION which occurs between the parts that are marked.

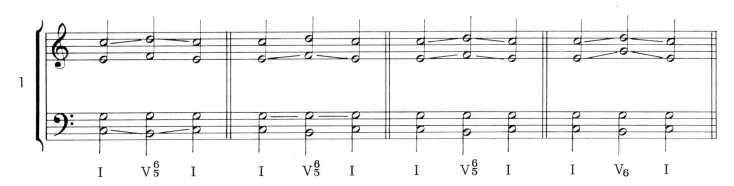

I   V$_5^6$ I   I   V$_5^6$ I   I   V$_5^6$ I   I   V$_6$ I

In Ex. 2 add the Alto and Bass parts to complete these chords. Try to avoid parallel Fifths and Octaves between any of the voices.

COME, HOLY SPIRIT   Simpson

I   I   V^7 IV$_6$ IV   I   IV$_4^6$ I   V   I   V   I   I   V

In Ex. 3 write two correct examples of these chord progressions to avoid the parallel Fifths and Octaves which appear here. You may change any notes except the Soprano.

Incorrect   Correct   Correct   Incorrect   Correct   Correct

V^7 I   V$_5^6$ I

In Ex. 4 harmonize the following melody with only I - IV - V - V^7 chords. Write the other three parts and mark the chord symbols below.

ARRANGING FOR VOICES

In learning to write four part choral arrangements (SATB) it is necessary to know the average range of each voice.

The interval between the Soprano-Alto and Alto-Tenor should stay within an octave. The Tenor and Bass parts may be more than an octave apart at times.

The 5th is omitted in the final chord to provide for better voice leading.

❋ In choral writing, when two or more eighth notes occur on a single syllable, they are usually connected by a BEAM (♫).

Music for four voices is often written on four staves in which case the Tenor part usually appears in the Treble Clef and sounds an octave lower than written.

❋ A slur is used to connect notes that move during a single syllable or word.

STUDENT ASSIGNMENT

Complete the next section of "Drink To Me Only With Thine Eyes" by adding the three lower voices as indicated by the chord symbols.

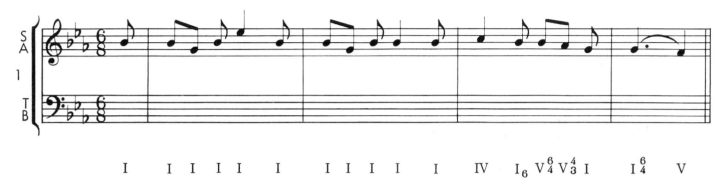

I   I I I I   I   I I I I   I   IV I_6 V^6_4 V^4_3 I I^6_4 V

In Ex. 2 the Soprano and Bass parts are given. Decide on the harmony you will use and write the chord symbols below the Bass; then add the Alto and Tenor parts.

Now write Ex. 2 on four staves with the Tenor part in the Treble Clef.

Soprano

Alto

3

Tenor

Bass

L-181

SECONDARY CHORDS

So far we have used the PRINCIPAL CHORDS of each key which are built on I – IV – V. Now let us examine the SECONDARY CHORDS which are built on II – III – VI – VII.

TRIADS IN C MAJOR

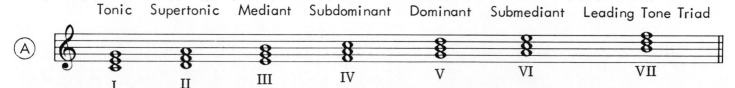

The Triad built on the second degree of the scale is called the SUPERTONIC.
The Triad built on the third degree of the scale is called the MEDIANT.
The Triad built on the sixth degree of the scale is called the SUBMEDIANT.

In any major key the II, III and VI Triads are <u>Minor Chords</u>. Each contains a Root, Minor Third and Perfect Fifth.

The Triad built on the seventh degree of the scale is called the LEADING TONE TRIAD.

This Triad contains a Root, Minor Third and Diminished Fifth. Therefore, it is called a DIMINISHED CHORD.

Here is an example of a four part arrangement which contains several SECONDARY CHORDS.

OLD HUNDREDTH

The following example contains all four SECONDARY CHORDS.

WELSH MELODY

REMEMBER:– Thus far we have used only the principal chords (I, IV, V or V^7) to harmonize a melody. (see MASTER THEORY Book 3, Lesson 85.) With the addition of the SECONDARY CHORDS the harmonic structure becomes much more interesting and varied.

STUDENT ASSIGNMENT

Date _____

Grade _____

1   Write the name of the following SECONDARY CHORDS. II_____

III_____VI _____VII _____

Write the Root Position, First Inversion and Second Inversion of the following SECONDARY CHORDS
in the Key of F Major. Keep all chords in close position.

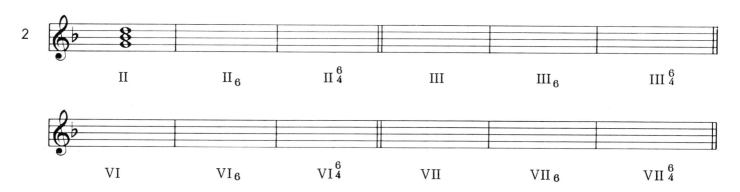

2

$$\text{II} \qquad \text{II}_6 \qquad \text{II}_4^6 \qquad \text{III} \qquad \text{III}_6 \qquad \text{III}_4^6$$

$$\text{VI} \qquad \text{VI}_6 \qquad \text{VI}_4^6 \qquad \text{VII} \qquad \text{VII}_6 \qquad \text{VII}_4^6$$

In Ex. 3 write the proper chord symbols, including inversions, under these SECONDARY CHORDS
in the Key of G Major.

3

VII

Ex. 4 contains a chord based on every degree of the G Major Scale. Analyze the harmony and
write in the chord symbols including any inversions.

PRAISE TO THE LORD

Gesangbuch

S
A

4

T
B

I

L-181

TRANSPOSING INSTRUMENTS

In writing for wind instruments, certain parts must be transposed to other keys. Instruments that sound where the music is written are said to be in CONCERT PITCH. These include:- Piccolo in C - Flute - Oboe - Bassoon - Trombone - Baritone (Bass Clef) - Basses.

B♭ INSTRUMENTS include:- B♭ Clarinet - B♭ Bass Clarinet - B♭ Tenor Saxophone - B♭ Cornet - B♭ Trumpet - Baritone (Treble Clef). Music for these instruments must be written in a key which is a MAJOR SECOND <u>higher</u> than Concert Pitch, <u>therefore</u>:- subtract two flats or add two sharps.

E♭ INSTRUMENTS include:- E♭ Clarinet - E♭ Alto Clarinet - E♭ Alto Saxophone - E♭ Baritone Saxophone - E♭ Alto Horn. Music for these instruments must be written in a key that is a MINOR THIRD <u>lower</u> than Concert Pitch, <u>therefore</u>:- subtract three flats or add three sharps.

<u>F INSTRUMENTS</u> include:- French Horn in F - English Horn. Music for these instruments must be written in a key that is a PERFECT FOURTH <u>lower</u> than Concert Pitch, <u>therefore</u>:- subtract one flat or add one sharp.

Here are the transpositions for all wind instruments.

AMERICA
Carey

STUDENT ASSIGNMENT

Date _____

Grade _____

The following melody is written in Concert Pitch. On the staff below, write the proper key signature and transpose this melody for B♭ INSTRUMENTS.

Transpose the following Concert Pitch melody for E♭ INSTRUMENTS.

Transpose the following Concert Pitch melody for F INSTRUMENTS.

3

4 The following letters represent the Major Keys in Concert Pitch. On the lines below, write the names of the proper Major Keys for transposing instruments in B♭, E♭ and F.

Concert Pitch	B♭	G	A♭	C	D	F	A	E♭
B♭ Instruments	C	—	—	—	—	—	—	—
E♭ Instruments	G	—	—	—	—	—	—	—
F Instruments	F	—	—	—	—	—	—	—

SAXOPHONE QUARTET

Now that we have learned to find the proper key for the transposing instruments, we must learn the actual sound of each in relation to Concert Pitch. For example, let us take the Saxophones:

(A) Music for the E♭ Alto Saxophone is written a MAJOR SIXTH <u>above</u> the actual sound.

(B) Music for the B♭ Tenor Saxophone is written ONE OCTAVE plus a MAJOR SECOND a-<u>bove</u> the actual sound.

(C) Music for the E♭ Baritone Saxophone is writ-ten ONE OCTAVE plus a MAJOR SIXTH a-<u>bove</u> the actual sound.

The S A T B arrangement of the first six bars of "America" is transposed below for Saxophone Quartet.

STUDENT ASSIGNMENT

Date _____

Grade _____

The notes in Ex. 1, 2 and 3 are written in concert pitch (actual sound). Transpose these exercises for the various Saxophones as indicated. Be sure to put in the correct key signatures.

Here are the last eight bars of "America" arranged for S A T B.

AMERICA (continued)

Now transpose the parts for Saxophone Quartet as we did in Lesson 49. Next, take four separate sheets of music paper and copy out the complete arrangement from Lessons 49 and 50 for Saxophone Quartet. This is your FIRST ARRANGEMENT, try to have it played.

AMERICA (continued)

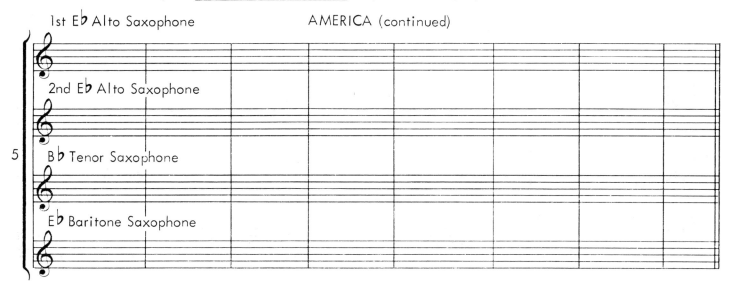

PASSING AND NEIGHBORING NOTES

A PASSING NOTE is a note that lies between two chord tones, but is not part of the chord. (Review Lesson 5 in Book 4, Master Theory, "Elementary Harmony".) It is marked Ⓟ. Here are some examples.

A MIGHTY FORTRESS

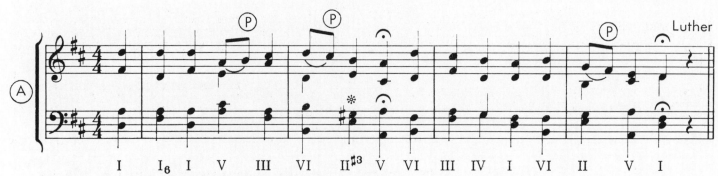

*Note the major third in the Supertonic Triad. This actually constitutes a temporary modulation to A Major.

A NEIGHBORING NOTE is a note lying immediately above or below a chord tone which returns to that tone. It is marked Ⓝ.

SUN OF MY SOUL

Passing and Neighboring Notes may also occur in more than one voice.

BATTLE HYMN OF THE REPUBLIC

STUDENT ASSIGNMENT

Date _____

Grade _____

Mark the PASSING NOTES Ⓟ and the NEIGHBORING NOTES Ⓝ in the following example.

THE OLD OAKEN BUCKET

Kaillmark

In Ex. 2 analyze the harmony, write the chord symbols below, and mark any Passing or Neighboring Notes.

THE FIRST NOEL

Traditional

Harmonize the melody in Ex. 3 using chords indicated by the chord symbols.   (No Passing or Neighboring Notes)

LONG, LONG AGO

Bayly

Now harmonize the same melody with only I and V^7 Chords as indicated, using Passing or Neighboring notes in one or more voices. Mark these notes Ⓟ or Ⓝ .

BRASS QUARTET

Date _____

Grade _____

For the purpose of this lesson the BRASS QUARTET will consist of: 1st B♭ Cornet, 2nd B♭ Cornet, Horn in F and Trombone.

(A) Music for the B♭ Cornet is written a MAJOR SECOND above the actual sound.

(B) Music for the Horn in F is written a PERFECT FIFTH above the actual sound.

(C) Music for the Trombone is written the same as the actual sound.

Analyze the harmony in the following four measures. Write the chord symbols underneath.

FOR THE BEAUTY OF THE EARTH

Kocher

Now arrange Ex. (D) for Brass Quartet as follows. Soprano = 1st B♭ Cornet, Alto = 2nd B♭ Cornet, Tenor = Horn in F, Bass = Trombone. Be sure to put in the correct key signature for each instrument.

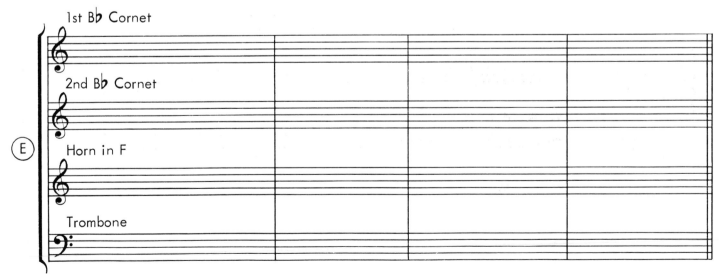

STUDENT ASSIGNMENT

Date _____

Grade _____

The notes in Ex. 1, 2 and 3 are written in Concert Pitch (actual sound). Write the Key Signature and transpose these examples for the Instruments indicated.

Music for Trombone is written in the Bass Clef and sounds as written.

Here are the last four bars of "For The Beauty Of The Earth". Analyze the harmony and write the Chord Symbols.

FOR THE BEAUTY OF THE EARTH (continued)

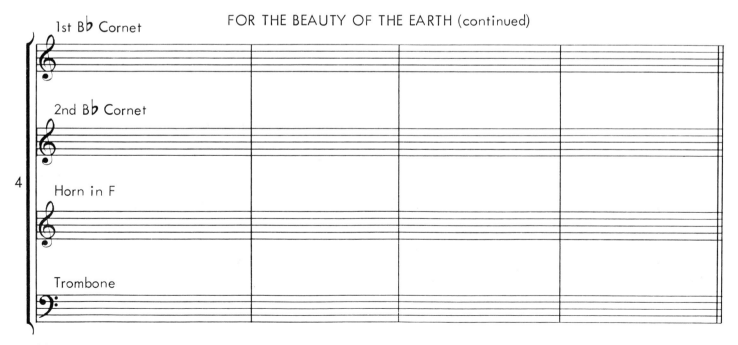

Arrange Ex. 3 for Brass Quartet. Next take four separate sheets of music paper, copy Ⓔ in Lesson 53 twice, then add the four bars below to complete the hymn. Try to have it played.

FOR THE BEAUTY OF THE EARTH (continued)

Lesson 55

CLARINET QUARTET

Date _____

Grade _____

The Clarinet Quartet in this lesson will include:- 1st B♭ Clarinet, 2nd B♭ Clarinet, E♭ Alto Clarinet and B♭ Bass Clarinet.

Ⓐ Music for the B♭ Clarinet is written a MAJOR SECOND <u>above</u> the actual sound.

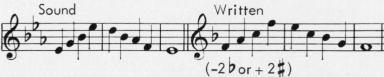

(−2♭ or +2♯)

Ⓑ Music for the E♭ Alto Clarinet is written a MAJOR SIXTH <u>above</u> the actual sound.

(−3♭ or +3♯)

Ⓒ Music for the B♭ Bass Clarinet is written ONE OCTAVE and a MAJOR SECOND <u>above</u> the actual sound.

(−2♭ or +2♯)

Analyze the harmony in Ex. Ⓓ . Write in the chord symbols and mark the Passing Ⓟ and Neighboring Ⓝ notes.

LONDONDERRY AIR

Arrange Ex. Ⓓ for Clarinet Quartet. Soprano = 1st B♭ Clarinet, Alto = 2nd B♭ Clarinet, Tenor = E♭ Alto Clarinet, Bass = B♭ Bass Clarinet. Check the key signatures carefully.

LONDONDERRY AIR

1st B♭ Clarinet

2nd B♭ Clarinet

Ⓔ E♭ Alto Clarinet

B♭ Bass Clarinet

STUDENT ASSIGNMENT

Date _____

Grade _____

Transpose Ex.1, 2 and 3 from Concert Pitch to the proper key for the Instruments listed.

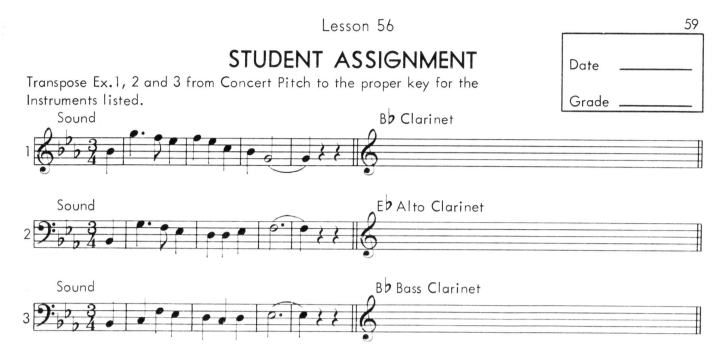

Here is the next part of "Londonderry Air". Analyze the harmony, write in the chord symbols and mark the Passing Ⓟ and Neighboring Ⓝ notes.

LONDONDERRY AIR (continued)

Arrange Ex.4 for Clarinet Quartet. Now combine this with the first portion in Lesson 55, Ex. Ⓔ and copy out the parts for the four Clarinets on separate sheets of paper. Try to have it played.

LONDONDERRY AIR (continued)

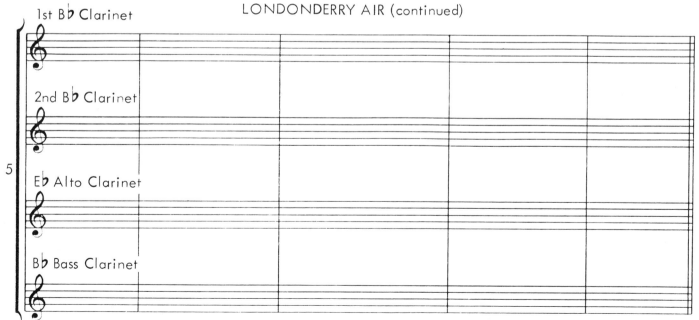

PIANO

Before concluding this book on Intermediate Harmony, we wish to make a brief reference to reading chords by letter names. Up to this point we have been mainly concerned with chord symbols ($I - I_6 - V^6_5$ etc.).

In the next book we will learn to make complete Band arrangements from Piano scores. Published Piano parts do not carry the chord symbols as we have been using them but usually have letter names of chords printed above the music. Here is an easy Piano part – single line melody with rhythmic accompaniment. Notice the Passing and Neighboring notes.

All chord names are written in Capital letters – single letters indicate Major chords. m = minor, + = augmented, dim. = diminished. Write a similar type of accompaniment to the following single line melody.

L-181

PIANO PARTS AND ASSIGNMENT

Here is an example of a rhythmic song written first for four voices
with chord symbols.

UP ON THE HOUSETOP   Hanby

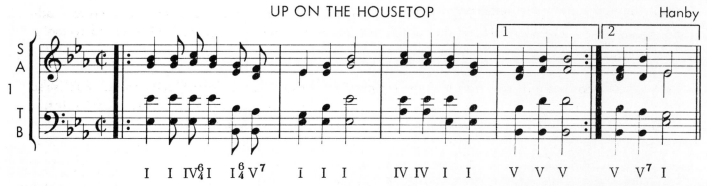

I   I   IV⁶₄I   I⁶₄V⁷   I   I   I   IV IV I   I   V   V   V   V V⁷ I

In Ex. 2 we have the same song adapted for Piano using letter names of chords for the harmonic
analysis.

Notice the single Bass notes above. These are always on chord tones but not usually on the same
note as the melody.

Here is the last portion of the same song. Write the letter names of the Chords above the music
and write a Bass Clef accompaniment in the style of Ex. 2.

UP ON THE HOUSETOP (continued)

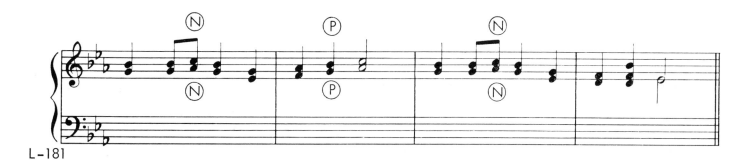

STUDENT TEST

Date _____

Grade _____

Lesson 31

1. The triad built on the first degree of the scale is called the_____.
2. The triad built on the fourth degree of the scale is called the_____.
3. The triad built on the fifth degree of the scale is called the_____.

4. Write the following chords in Close Position.

5. Write the following chords in Open Position.

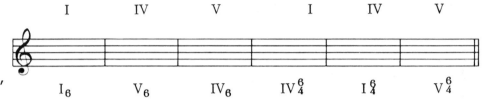

Lesson 33

1. Write the following Inversions in the Key of C Major, Close Position.

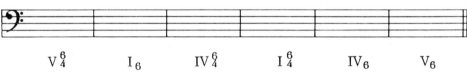

2. Write the following Inversions in the Key of C Major, Open Position.

Lesson 35

1. Analyze the harmony and write the Chord Symbols below this hymn.

2. Name the interval of the chord which is doubled at (X)_____ (Y)_____ (Z)_____.

3. Name the interval of the chord which is omitted at ✳ _____.

Lesson 36

Fill in the ALTO (stems down) and TENOR (stems up) to complete these chords.

Lesson 37

Write these inversions of the V⁷ Chord in Close Position.

STUDENT TEST

Date _____

Grade _____

Lesson 39

Analyze the harmony and write in the Chord Symbols.

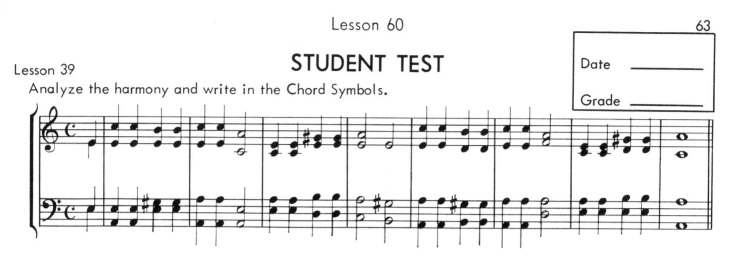

Lesson 43 – Add the three lower voices as indicated by the Chord Symbols.

I V$_2^4$ I$_6$ V$_3^4$ I V$_2^4$ I$_6$ IV V V I

Lesson 45 – Analyze the harmony and write the Chord Symbols below.

Lesson 47

The following melody is written for C Instruments in Concert Pitch. In 2-3 and 4, write the key signature and transpose for the Instruments listed.

L-181

STUDENT TEST

Date _____

Grade _____

Lesson 49

1. Analyze the harmony and write in the Chord Symbols.

2. Arrange the above example for the Brass Quartet listed below.

1st B♭ Cornet

2nd B♭ Cornet

Horn in F

Trombone

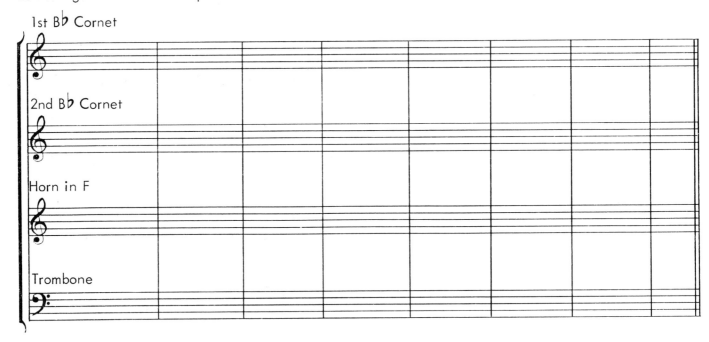

Lesson 57

Write a rhythmic accompaniment in the Bass Clef to complete the following Piano Part.

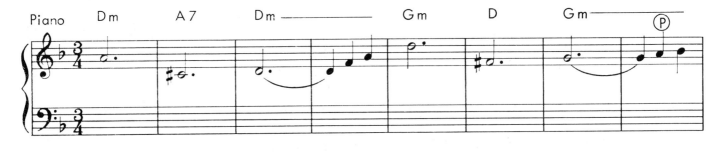